YOU CHOOSE

DARING SEA EVACUATION AT DUNKIRK

INTERACTIVE WORLD WAR II MISSIONS

by Jessica Gunderson

CAPSTONE PRESS
a capstone imprint

Published by Capstone Press, an imprint of Capstone
1710 Roe Crest Drive, North Mankato, Minnesota 56003
capstonepub.com

Library of Congress Cataloging-in-Publication Data
is available on the Library of Congress website.

ISBN: 9798875244612 (hardcover)
ISBN: 9798875244582 (paperback)
ISBN: 9798875244599 (ebook PDF)

Summary: You are taking part in the daring evacuation of stranded soldiers from Dunkirk, in northern France, during World War II. In this interactive adventure, YOU CHOOSE the paths that will lead you and others to freedom or spell your doom!

Editorial Credits
Editor: Alison Deering; Designer: Bobbie Nuytten; Media Researcher: Svetlana Zhurkin; Production Specialist: Katy LaVigne

Image Credits
Alamy: piemags/archive/military, 108 (bottom), Volgi archive, 59; DVIDS: NARA, 64; Getty Images: Arkivi, 104, bloodua, 84, Hulton Archive, 38, Hulton Archive/Keystone, 8, 12, 14, 42, 74, 102, Hulton Archive/Picture Post, 25, 67, Jens Deppner, 33, Keystone/Bert Hardy, 30, Stocktrek Images/Mark Stevenson, cover (top), 95, Topical Press Agency/Davis, 40; NARA: U.S. Air Force, 78; Shutterstock: Buch and Bee (airplane emblem), 5 and throughout, Everett Collection, 4, 50, jollys_art (old paper), cover and throughout, Keith Tarrier, 108 (top), Pablo Caridad (paper file), 1 and throughout, ploy2907, 6–7, Valentin Agapov (folder), back cover and throughout; SuperStock: Image Asset Management/World History Archive, 47, 89, Pantheon/Mary Evans Picture Library, cover (bottom), PL Photography Limited/Piemags, 100

Printed and bound in China. 6461

TABLE OF CONTENTS

Thousands of troops wait for evacuation on the beaches of Dunkirk.

ABOUT YOUR ADVENTURE

YOU are about to experience one of the largest rescue operations of World War II. In May 1940, more than 300,000 British and French soldiers were pushed to the French coast and trapped near the seaside city of Dunkirk. Nazi forces surged toward them on one side. On the other side lay the English Channel. The soldiers had nowhere to go.

You could be a British soldier, pursued by Germans and trapped on the beaches near Dunkirk. Or you might be a British sailor, maneuvering across the Channel to rescue trapped soldiers. You could be a pilot in the Royal Air Force (RAF), fighting off German planes to protect soldiers on the beaches. Wherever you are, your choices might mean your survival or your death.

Turn the page to begin your adventure.

OPERATION DYNAMO

Operation Dynamo was a rescue mission to evacuate more than 300,000 Allied troops from northern France. When German Nazi forces invaded the country, they pushed the British Expeditionary Forces (BEF), along with French and Belgian units, west toward the sea. The troops became trapped on the beaches of Dunkirk.

The British Royal Navy sent more than 1,000 ships—both Navy and civilian—to rescue the Allied soldiers. The ships left from Ramsgate in Kent, England. Sailing across the English Channel to France, the ships braved attacks from German fighter pilots, the Luftwaffe. The ships loaded up with soldiers and sailed back to England. The rescue continued until nearly all soldiers were evacuated.

ENGLAND

ENGLISH CHANNEL

Key Terms

Allies—France and Great Britain; later included the United States, Soviet Union, and China

Axis powers—Germany, Italy, and Japan

English Channel—a narrow strip of sea separating northern France from southern England

Luftwaffe—German Air Force

When:

The rescue took place from May 26–June 4, 1940.

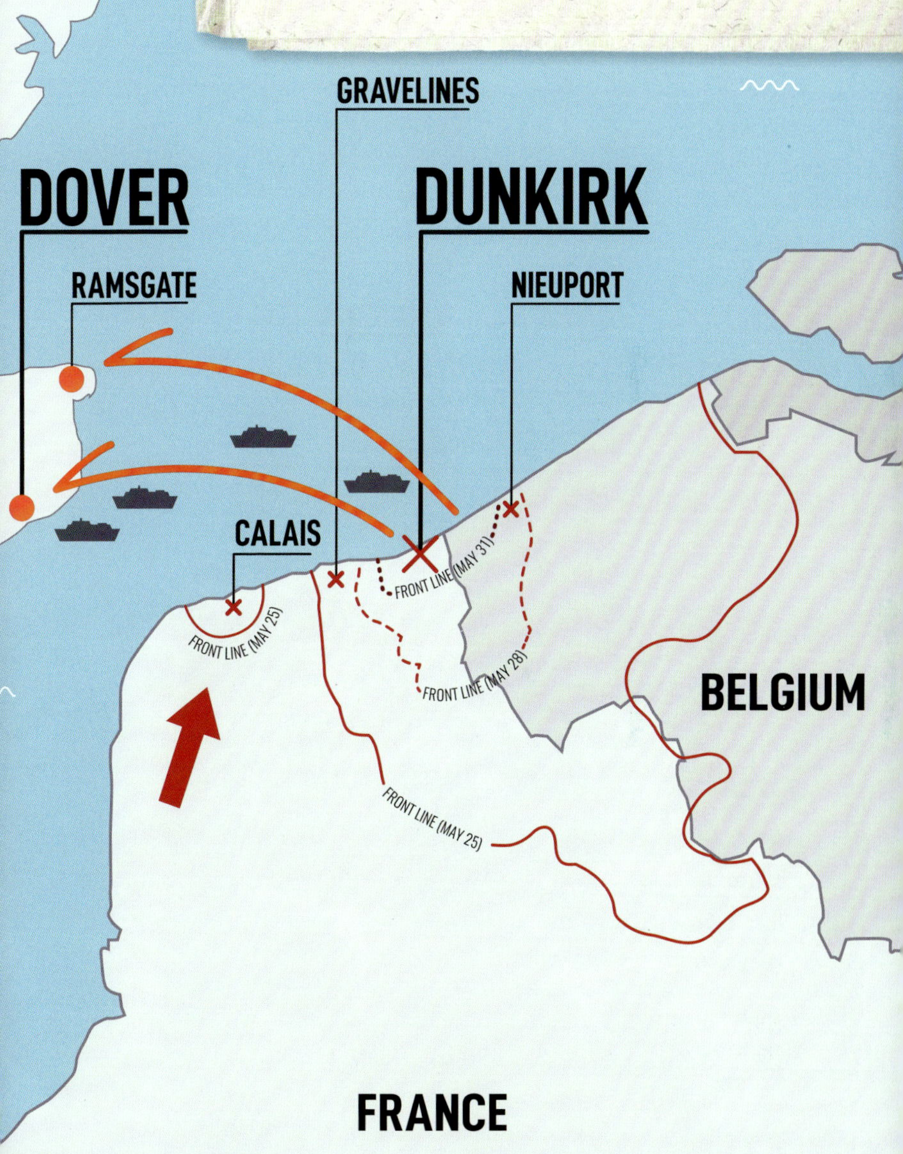

Chapter 1
TRAPPED IN FRANCE

When Adolf Hitler rises to power in 1930s Germany, the world watches in dismay. Hitler declares himself a dictator and passes laws against Jewish people. Then, in 1939, Hitler's Nazi forces invade Poland. On September 3, 1939, Great Britain and France declare war on Germany. World War II begins.

Britain sends the British Expeditionary Forces (BEF) to help defend France from Hitler's advancing troops. The British and French become known as the Allied powers.

The Allied forces are ready for Hitler's invasion. They build up defenses along the Maginot Line, a defensive barrier in northeast France that separates Germany and France.

But the Nazis don't invade across the Maginot Line. Instead, in May 1940, they invade Belgium. They enter France through the Ardennes Forest, going around the Maginot Line.

The Allies fight to hold off the Nazis, but the Nazis push them back. They drive the Allies toward the northwest coast of France, surrounding them. With the ocean on one side and the Nazis on the other, more than 300,000 Allied soldiers are trapped.

The British military commanders understand that if their army can't be saved, the Germans will continue invading Europe. England will likely be next. They must find a way to evacuate the Allied soldiers from the French coast.

So, from a room deep inside Dover Castle, located in Kent, England, the British launch Operation Dynamo. The plan is to order the troops to retreat to Dunkirk, on the coast of France.

After days of secretive planning, Operation Dynamo begins on May 26, 1940. The British Royal Navy sends as many ships as possible to rescue the soldiers. The RAF will provide air support against the German Luftwaffe. But the Navy cannot rescue the stranded soldiers without help. They also need civilian boats. Called "The Little Ships of Dunkirk," these civilian crafts—yachts, pleasure boats, fishing vessels, barges, and cruise ships—will sail across the English Channel to Dunkirk, braving Nazi attacks from above.

Can thousands of soldiers be evacuated from Nazi-occupied France? Only then will the Allies have a chance to win the war. How will you experience the daring sea rescue?

To be a British soldier on the shores of France, turn to page 13.

To be a civilian in command of a Little Ship, turn to page 43.

To be a pilot in the Royal Air Force, turn to page 75.

Chapter 2

ESCAPE FROM DUNKIRK

The woods are thick, and the road is uneven with craters caused by German Nazi bombs. You are careful not to stumble as you walk, scanning the woods for Germans who may be lurking behind the trees.

You signed up for the British army months ago when the war began. The Allied Forces prepared for the Nazi invasion into France. You and your fellow soldiers helped build up the Maginot Line.

But then, the Nazis surprised everyone by invading France through the thick Ardennes Forest instead. They advanced with their heavy tanks called panzers, blasting through the woods and pushing the Allied Forces back.

Turn the page.

Now you are under orders to retreat to the seaside city of Dunkirk, France. Nazi attacks have taken out most of your numbers. Your unit is just a small group of four grubby soldiers—Pete, George, Henry, and you. Worse, you have no weapons.

"Get down!" Henry hisses suddenly.

You crouch, and then you hear it—the whirring of a plane overhead. It's a Stuka, a German dive-bomber plane, part of the Nazi's powerful air force, the Luftwaffe. They have dropped bombs all over France.

World War II-era German Stuka dive-bombers

The roar of the German bomber fades, and you stand up and continue on.

"What's in Dunkirk anyway?" you ask. "It's on the sea. We'll be trapped there, with Germans behind us and nowhere to go."

"The commanders must have a plan," Henry says, shrugging again. "But my plan now is to find some food."

Your stomach rumbles at the words. You are hungry too. You have no food and little water. Yesterday, Pete killed a rabbit on the roadside and roasted it over a fire. It was the only food you had in days. The memory of the cooked meat makes your mouth water and your knees weak.

"How much farther to Dunkirk?" you wonder aloud.

But Henry isn't listening. "Look!" he says, pointing.

Turn the page.

You follow his gaze and see a farmhouse nestled in the trees.

"It looks abandoned," you say.

"Probably," agrees Pete. "Most of the French civilians have fled."

"Should we check it out?" George asks. "We could rest there, and maybe find some food."

"I don't know," you say. "We need to get to Dunkirk as soon as possible. If we stop, the Germans might catch up to us."

"But we need rest to keep going," Henry argues.

He might be right. You do need rest. Your boots are worn thin, and your legs weak and sore. But you are worried about the Germans and want to reach Dunkirk as soon as possible.

To stop and check out the farmhouse, go to page 17.

To convince the others to keep going, turn to page 19.

"Let's check out the farmhouse," you say. "If there's nothing there, we'll keep moving."

You and your fellow soldiers approach the farmhouse, scanning the area for any enemies who may be lurking. But nothing stirs.

Oiaaaah! The scream is loud and inhuman. Startled, you drop to the ground. Henry drops beside you too. *Squeee!*

Pete laughs as he looks down at you. "It's a pig, you guys!"

You stand, brushing yourself off. "I'm from London," you say. "We don't have live pigs in the city."

"I'm so hungry I could eat that *whole* pig," Henry says. He points to the farmhouse. "No one has come out yet. It must be abandoned."

Sure enough, as you approach the house, no one emerges. Inside, the fireplace is still warm. The family must have just left.

Turn the page.

Pete roasts one of the pigs, and you have a nice supper. The four of you take turns keeping watch while the others sleep.

Early in the morning, you set out toward Dunkirk. As dawn breaks, you feel nervous. You can still hear gunfire—the sounds are even closer than yesterday

Henry seems to read your thoughts. "The road is dangerous," he says, motioning to a swath of land beyond the trees. "We should find another way. How about crossing that field?"

"The field looks waterlogged," George says. "It will take too long."

To stay on the road, turn to page 21.

To cross the field, turn to page 22.

The road is dangerous, but it's the quickest way to get to Dunkirk. "We need to keep going," you say.

George nods in agreement. Henry sighs but he doesn't argue.

You continue along the road. Then, from out of nowhere, a German plane zooms above you. Before you have time to react, a blast throws you into the ditch.

When you come to, Henry and the others are gone. Maybe they were captured. Or maybe they thought you were dead. Either way, you're alone now.

Your ankle is throbbing, and blood spurts from a wound on your arm. You hobble along the road, scanning the woods for any lurking enemies.

In a nearby ditch, sunlight glints on metal. You hurry toward the object. It's an abandoned bicycle. What luck! You hop on and speed

Turn the page.

toward Dunkirk. As you draw closer, you spy clouds of smoke rising from the city. The port of Dunkirk is in flames.

You cycle toward a group of British soldiers. "Where are you headed?" you ask.

"The beaches," one tells you. "The Royal Navy is going to evacuate us."

A rescue plan? The other soldier's words are welcome news. You toss the bicycle and join the others.

On the beach, thousands of British soldiers are gathered, waiting to be rescued. Some are lined up along the sand banks. Others are standing on the mole, a long pier that juts out into the sea.

"Choose a line and get in," a soldier says.

To get in line on the mole, turn to page 24.

To head to the sand banks, turn to page 26.

"The sooner we get to Dunkirk, the better," you say. "Let's stay on the road."

You keep moving. Soon, the salty smell of the sea fills the air.

"We must be getting close to Dunkirk," you say excitedly to Henry.

"Yes. I wonder—" His words are cut off by the roar of a Stuka overhead.

"Scatter and get down!" Henry cries.

You leap into the ditch and cover your head. The Stuka swoops, dropping a bomb right next to where you lay. Your final wish is that your fellow soldiers survived the bombing and will make it to Dunkirk.

THE END

To follow another path, turn to page 11.
To learn more about the Miracle of Dunkirk, turn to page 103.

The field is waterlogged, but it's better than risking your life on the road. You trudge across the wet ground. Finally, you smell salt in the air. You are nearing the sea!

When you reach the beaches of Dunkirk, you are shocked to see thousands of people. Lines of soldiers snake along the sand.

"The British Navy is sending ships to evacuate us," one of the soldiers tells you. "But you gotta wait in line. First come, first served."

A beachmaster directs you to the back of the line. Little ships ferry soldiers from the beach to larger ships, but the process is slow. Your line barely moves. Time creeps by.

One day passes, then another. You try to ration your food, but soon it is gone. Drinking water is scarce. You grow weak and tired. Stukas scream overhead. Falling to the sand and covering your head at the sight of planes becomes routine. Delirium sets in.

One morning, you look around, perplexed. You're unable to remember why you're on the beach in the first place.

Henry seems equally confused. Suddenly, he points to the sea. "I can see England! Let's swim home."

It hits you then—you're waiting to be rescued. But why wait when you could swim?

Henry tugs your arm. "Come on, let's go!"

A soldier ahead of you in line turns around. "You're delirious!" he says. "The Channel is at least 40 miles across at this point!"

"If we can see it, we can swim to it," Henry insists.

You try to think clearly. Henry could be right. Waiting around for a rescue that might never come isn't doing you any good. But the water might be dangerous.

To join Henry and swim, turn to page 29.

To stay in line, turn to page 30.

You decide to join the line on the mole. As you make your way there, a screech pierces your ears. A Stuka swoops through the sky.

You fling yourself to the sand. The ground beneath you rumbles as the bomb hits. When the plane is gone, you sit up. The bomb landed down the beach, and you are lucky to be far from the impact. Everyone shuffles quietly back into line.

You wait for hours, but finally, three steamers arrive. You are about to climb onto one when bombers fly overhead. You drop down and cover your head as explosions sound around you.

When all is silent, you look up to see two of the steamers destroyed—including the one you were about to board.

You sigh in dismay. Thousands of soldiers are still waiting, and now only one steamer—the HMS *Crested Eagle*—remains intact.

Soldiers line the sand dunes at Dunkirk as they await evacuation.

You get in line again, but the *Crested Eagle* is almost full.

"Only one spot left!" the boarding officer shouts.

You are about to board, when you notice a wounded soldier behind you.

You could give him your spot and wait for another rescue ship. But you are eager to get off this beach and back to England.

To board the *Crested Eagle*, turn to page 32.

To let the other soldier board and wait, turn to page 34.

The line on the mole is long, so you decide to join the soldiers waiting near the sand banks. But the lines are long here too. The small boats can only ferry a couple dozen soldiers at a time out to the big vessels.

"It'll be days before I get out of here," you mutter to yourself.

"I was just thinking the same thing," says a man behind you. He has a thick French accent. He introduces himself as Pierre. "I was separated from my unit."

"Me too," you say. "Let's buddy up."

You and Pierre make your way down the beach. You try not to notice the bodies of fallen soldiers lying in the sand.

Suddenly, Pierre clutches your arm. "Hear that?" he says. "A Stuka dive-bomber!"

Sure enough, you hear the screech of the plane's engine as it streams into sight.

"Quick, get down!" Pierre says. "Pull one of the fallen soldiers over you."

You hesitate for a second, then do as he says. Bullets from the Stuka's guns rain down. Then a blast shakes the ground. Sand and shrapnel rain down, but you are protected by the soldier.

When all is clear, you stand up. "Thanks, Pierre," you say.

He nods. "That blast could've seriously injured us," he says. "Let's keep going down the beach. Maybe we can find some water or food."

As you walk, you notice a group of soldiers gathered in a circle. "Looks like they're building something," you say.

"Let's check it out," Pierre suggests.

One of the soldiers looks up as you approach. "We're building a raft," he says. "We could use a couple more hands."

Turn the page.

"We're going to float out to the steamers. No time to wait around for the ferries," another soldier adds.

"We'll gladly help," says Pierre.

The first soldier eyes Pierre suspiciously. Then he shakes his head. "Just you," he says, pointing at you. "Only British on this raft."

"But we're on the same side!" Pierre exclaims.

The soldiers simply glare at him. Pierre looks at you. You can't meet his eyes.

"I'll go then," he says.

"Wait!" you say.

Pierre just helped save your life. You should stick with him. But you don't want to lose your chance of rescue.

To leave with Pierre, turn to page 39.

To stay and help the soldiers build the raft, turn to page 41.

Waiting around is driving you mad. You need to do *something.*

"Let's go," you tell Henry.

You both step out of line and head toward the water. The dark strip on the horizon looks even closer now.

Henry's eyes are glassy as he stares at water. "Home," he murmurs, rushing forward.

You follow, stripping off your shirt so it doesn't weigh you down. At first, swimming is easy. But soon, your limbs tire. Exhaustion—caused by lack of food and sleep—sets in. You can't see Henry anymore, either.

As hard as you swim, England doesn't get any closer. There are no boats around to rescue you, either. As you succumb to the sea, you realize your deadly mistake.

THE END

To follow another path, turn to page 11.
To learn more about the Miracle of Dunkirk, turn to page 103.

You want to get home more than anything, but you know you are too exhausted to swim one mile, let alone 21.

"No, Henry," you say. "We'll never make it."

He stares at the horizon, his eyes watery with either tears or delirium. "But . . ."

"No," you repeat.

Suddenly, Henry bolts toward the water. You try to grab him, but he's out of reach.

"Stop!" a beachmaster shouts. He pulls out his gun and points it at Henry. "I have orders to shoot anyone who steps out of line!"

Soldiers trudge through the water to get to waiting ships during the Dunkirk rescue.

Henry lowers his head and trudges back into line.

For days, you wait in line. Thankfully, clouds roll in—they prevent Nazi planes from divebombing the beach. Small boats come to shore, ferrying soldiers to larger ships. Slowly, the line inches forward.

On the final day, you wait in waist-deep water. The water is cold, and you feel numb. But you don't complain and neither do the others, not even Henry.

Finally, a little ship picks you up and takes you to one of the Royal Navy destroyers. On the ship, you and Henry warm up by the boilers. Before you know it, you are home. England. You've survived and are ready to fight again when the time comes.

THE END

To follow another path, turn to page 11.
To learn more about the Miracle of Dunkirk, turn to page 103.

Before you can speak, the wounded man does. “I’ll wait for the next ship,” he says.

Relieved, you board the *Crested Eagle*. At the front of the ship are lounges where soldiers have gathered. But they are too full, so you stand in one of the narrow halls instead. The ship sets off, and you are finally on your way to England.

You’ve only been at sea for a few minutes when suddenly, the ship lurches. You are knocked against the wall.

The ship sways again. *Boom!* A bomb drops, lighting up the front of the vessel. You can feel the heat from the flames. The ship is on fire!

You push through the hall to the starboard side as the *Crested Eagle* rocks again. Out here, the flames are thick, reaching up to the sky like red tongues. Around you, soldiers are yelling and flinging themselves into the water.

The wreckage of the *Crested Eagle*

You have no choice. You grab hold of the railing and throw yourself into the water, sinking down into its depths.

When you surface, you paddle breathlessly and look around. There are men clinging to lifeboats, but the boats are nearly full. You aren't too far from the beach. You can make out the lines of men standing in the water. You could either swim to a lifeboat or paddle toward the shore.

To swim to a lifeboat, turn to page 36.

To paddle to the beach, turn to page 37.

You desperately want to be evacuated, but you know the wounded soldier needs to be rescued more than you.

"Take my spot," you tell him.

You wait for hours, although it feels more like days. German planes whiz overhead. You and the others crouch. The mole shakes as bombs explode in the water. But the mole is unhit.

Finally, you board a passenger ferry. It is a large vessel that holds thousands. But such a big boat is an easy target for the Nazi bombers.

An hour into the journey, six German bombers zoom through the sky, shelling the ferry. One bomb hits, dropping straight through the boat and leaving a giant hole on the starboard side.

"Gather on the port side!" the officer calls.

You and the other soldiers move to the port side of the boat. The boat raises out of the water enough so the Navy sailors can patch the hole using mattresses and pieces of wood.

Then, the ferry is on its way again. You get off the boat at the seaside port of Ramsgate, England, safe and ready to return to war when you are called up again.

THE END

To follow another path, turn to page 11.
To learn more about the Miracle of Dunkirk, turn to page 103.

You swim toward one of the lifeboats. It looks full, but you're willing to take a chance. Surely the boat can fit one more.

"Help!" you call as you near the boat. You wave one arm as you paddle with the other.

"Come aboard!" one soldier calls.

"The boat is too full!" another soldier argues.

You swim toward the boat anyway. Strong arms pull you up, and you gasp for breath, relieved.

But your relief lasts only a second. With your weight, the boat sways, then tips, spilling you and the others into the water. As you fall, your head knocks against the side of the boat. Unconscious, you sink to your watery grave.

THE END

To follow another path, turn to page 11.
To learn more about the Miracle of Dunkirk, turn to page 103.

You don't want to risk swimming to a lifeboat, only to be turned away because it is too full. Instead, you splash toward the shore. But the beach is farther away than it appears.

You float on your back for a few minutes to gain strength. As you stare up at the sky, you see a familiar sight—a German bomber. Before you can take another breath, a bomb explodes in the water, knocking you out cold.

When you wake, you are lying on the beach. You try to call out, but your voice is weak and muffled. You can't stand up either. Your leg might be broken.

You collapse into the sand. Hours later, you are abruptly awakened by rough hands grasping your arms.

"Oh, thank goodness," you say.

But when you swivel your head to look at your savior, your heart lunges to your throat. The soldier wears the Nazi symbol on his arm.

Turn the page.

The soldier shouts something in German, and other Nazi soldiers rush toward you. You are loaded onto a cart and carried off.

British and French soldiers taken prisoner by German forces

For the rest of the war, you are a prisoner of war in a Nazi camp. You and the other prisoners have little to eat, and the Nazi guards are stern and cruel. Even though you live through your experience, your time as prisoner haunts you for the rest of your days.

THE END

To follow another path, turn to page 11.
To learn more about the Miracle of Dunkirk, turn to page 103.

You don't want to abandon Pierre. Plus, the raft might not make it out to one of the steamers anyway.

You turn to the soldiers. "Sorry. I'm sticking with him," you say.

Pierre smiles gratefully as you move off down the beach. "Our best chance is to get into line," he says.

You agree, and for the next two days, the two of you wait. The line moves slowly, but finally it is your chance to board a small boat. It carries you to a Navy steamer. Soon, you are chugging across the English Channel to Ramsgate, England.

In Ramsgate, you and Pierre say your goodbyes. He will wait in Ramsgate for orders from the French Army, and you will go home to your family for a few days' leave.

At first, you are worried you and the others at Dunkirk will be considered failures for

Turn the page.

British soldiers arrive back in London, England, following evacuation from Dunkirk.

fleeing the advancing Germans. But instead, you are greeted with cheers. The Dunkirk Evacuation becomes a major turning point in the war. More than 338,000 soldiers have been saved, and the British Army is ready to continue the fight against the Axis powers. You are proud to be one of them.

THE END

To follow another path, turn to page 11.
To learn more about the Miracle of Dunkirk, turn to page 103.

You know it is rude to leave Pierre to fend for himself, but you need to save yourself. The raft is your best and quickest option.

"I'll help build the raft," you tell the soldiers.

With driftwood and some found twine, you and the soldiers piece together a makeshift raft. At first, you don't think it will hold, but the raft is sturdy.

You and the group of soldiers float to a steamer, where you are pulled aboard. The steamer takes you to England, where you rest for a few days before rejoining the war effort.

Every time you think of Dunkirk, you are happy you survived, but you feel guilty about Pierre. You hope he made it out alive too.

THE END

To follow another path, turn to page 11.
To learn more about the Miracle of Dunkirk, turn to page 103.

Chapter 3

OPERATION DYNAMO

The day is bright and sunny—a perfect day for sailing. Spending time on your family's yacht is your favorite pastime. There's not much else to do on your estate in rural Kent, England. You often take the boat out of Ramsgate into the English Channel.

You don your sailing gear and head downstairs to your father's study. He looks up at you as you enter.

"No sailing today," he says, his face grim. "Our yacht has been requisitioned for the war."

"Requisitioned?" you repeat.

"The Royal Navy is going to use it for a secret naval operation," he explains.

You are stunned but intrigued. When Great Britain and France declared war on Germany

Turn the page.

in September 1939, the British government sent the BEF to France. In May 1940, Hitler's forces invaded Belgium and France.

The BEF and other Allied Forces have battled courageously. But Hitler's troops have continued to advance. The newspapers don't tell everything, and you know there is more to the story.

"If our yacht is joining the war effort, then so am I!" you say.

Before your father can argue, you head to the nearest naval office and sign up. You are a strong sailor, so you don't need much training. After a few quick days of preparation with other recruits, you are ready.

When you report to your commander, he looks at your training record. "You are familiar with sailing yachts," he says. "And you know the English Channel well."

"Yes, sir," you say.

"The German invasion forced the Allies to retreat to the beaches of Dunkirk, France," he tells you. "More than 300,000 soldiers are trapped there with nowhere to go. We are sending boats in the area to evacuate them."

So that's why your yacht was needed!

"We'd like you to be part of the rescue," the commander continues. "Operation Dynamo."

You know the task is dangerous, but you are up for it. "Yes, sir!" you agree.

"We need someone to sail one of the civilian yachts. And we also need sailors on the large Navy destroyers."

You hesitate. Sailing a yacht is a huge responsibility—and dangerous. German aircraft could undoubtedly sink a civilian boat. But sailing on a Navy ship is dangerous too. The Nazis could easily spot a destroyer from the air.

To sail a yacht, turn to page 46.

To be assigned to a large naval ship, turn to page 48.

You have been sailing all your life for pleasure. Now is the time to sail for a real purpose—to rescue British soldiers.

You and another sailor, Williams, are taken to one of the yachts in Ramsgate harbor. You take the helm and set off across the English Channel. Five other civilian vessels—larger yachts, a ferry, and a barge—follow after you.

The seaway is familiar, but you know at any time, you could be attacked from above. The Luftwaffe are ferocious. Their Stukas—German dive-bomber planes—and Messerschmitts—long-range bomber planes—are dangerous threats. Plus, German submarines have laid mines all along the Channel.

Still, you continue on. Suddenly, you see smoke up ahead.

"A ship is on fire!" Williams exclaims.

As you draw closer, you see that soldiers are flailing in the water.

The Little Ships of Dunkirk were key to evacuating British soldiers and other Allied troops from the beaches of Dunkirk.

"We need to rescue them," you say.

"The other ships behind us have more space," Williams argues.

The water is slick with oil. At any moment, the oil could ignite. A small boat like yours would be engulfed in flames immediately. And Williams is right—the other ships are larger with more men. But your conscience nags at you anyway.

To let another ship come to the soldiers' rescue, turn to page 50.

To save the soldiers in the water, turn to page 52.

You are assigned to the crew of the HMS *Basilisk*. The massive naval destroyer can hold thousands of men. You are grateful to be on it.

You set off across the Channel. As the ship nears Dunkirk, a sudden sound pierces the air. German bombers whiz overhead.

As the planes close in, they begin firing at the destroyer. You drop to the deck, covering your head, as the destroyer's gunners fire back.

Sploosh! A bomb hits the water nearby. Then the bombers disappear into the clouds.

When the destroyer starts moving again, the commander calls to you.

"The destroyer is too large to get close to the beach," he tells you. "We're sending lifeboats to gather soldiers. Pick up as many as you can, and bring them back to the ship."

You and a sailor named Rashad climb into a lifeboat. The waves around you are littered with floating objects—guns, ammunition, and broken pieces of watercraft.

Soldiers splash toward you. Overhead, another German Stuka screams. The soldiers duck underwater, and you and Rashad flatten to the bottom of the lifeboat. The Stuka whizzes past, dropping its bomb farther up the shore.

You help pull several soldiers into the lifeboat and take them to the destroyer. After several trips, you are exhausted. So is Rashad.

"Let's call it a night," he says.

You look back toward the lines of soldiers on the beach. There are so many still waiting.

"Just one more trip!" you respond.

Rashad shakes his head. "We need rest."

You know there is more room on the *Basilisk*. But you and Rashad are in this together. Maybe you should listen to him.

To make one more trip, turn to page 59.

To go back to the ship, turn to page 69.

As you pass by the wreck, you see Williams is right. There are too many sailors in the water. You don't have room for them all. Plus, another boat behind you is already veering toward the fiery ship.

With the wreckage behind you, you continue toward Dunkirk. The faster you get there, the more soldiers you can save.

Suddenly, a low rumble like thunder comes from overhead. You look up to see a plane darting through the sky.

"Is that friendly or enemy?" you ask.

German Stuka dive-bombers fly in formation during WWII.

As the words leave your mouth, the plane speeds up. Looking up, you see gull-like wings—it's a German Stuka bomber. Your heart pounds. There's no way you can outrun the Stuka.

"Get below deck!" you shout to Williams.

Bam! The shock of impact sends you flailing backward. The scream of the plane fizzles to a whimper as it zooms out of sight.

"We've been hit!" Williams cries as he emerges from below deck.

"How bad is it?" you ask.

"The hull is cracked," he says.

You inspect the damage. The hull is splintered and slowly filling with water. The yacht needs to be repaired quickly or it will sink. You could turn back to Ramsgate. You know you'll be able to find someone to repair the yacht quickly. Or you could continue on to Dunkirk. But you don't know what to expect there.

To turn back, turn to page 55.

To keep going to Dunkirk, turn to page 57.

You can't leave the soldiers to drown. After all, you are here to save as many as you can.

You weave through the water toward the flaming vessel. The water is slick and oily. You and Williams pull the soldiers from the water and onto the yacht. Some of the men are nearly unconscious. Others are burned. Many need medical attention. And all are crammed tightly into the small yacht.

As you sail away from the wreckage, a spark from the vessel ignites the oil. Flames lick the air. You were lucky to arrive when you did.

"We need to go back to Ramsgate," you say. "These men need care."

"We should keep going," Williams says. "We can bring them to a medical ship in Dunkirk."

To go back to Ramsgate, go to page 53.

To keep going to Dunkirk, turn to page 65.

"These soldiers will receive care faster if we take them back to England," you say, turning the yacht toward Ramsgate.

The day is gray and cloudy. You scan the sky for enemy planes that may be hidden among the clouds. Before you see anything, you hear the siren. It's a Stuka!

"Get down!" you cry.

You hold the wheel, shielding your head, but no bombs drop. Instead, the Stuka lifts up into the air and disappears into the clouds.

"Probably couldn't see us with all the clouds," Williams says.

Relieved, you turn back to steering. Finally, the Ramsgate harbor appears through the fog.

"Injured soldiers on board!" you shout as pull in.

A medical boat with a red cross on it zooms toward you. You help load the injured soldiers

Turn the page.

onto the boat. You know they will get the care they need.

After the yacht has been emptied, you refuel and set off again across the Channel. Other small watercrafts, along with larger Navy vessels, are making their way across.

When you reach Dunkirk, you see soldiers up and down the beaches, as far as you can see.

"How can we save them all?" you exclaim. "We're such a small boat."

"Every little bit counts," Williams says.

You nod in agreement. Then, you hear shouts from the boats around you. You look up to see a German Stuka dive-bomber overhead. Your voice joins the chorus of shouts, but you are quickly silenced when the bomb drops on your yacht. As you go down with the boat, you hope the other rescue boats are more successful.

THE END

To follow another path, turn to page 11.
To learn more about the Miracle of Dunkirk, turn to page 103.

"We can't rescue anyone with a broken boat," you admit. "We'll have to get it repaired in Ramsgate."

Williams agrees, and you turn the boat around. As you near the harbor, the engine chugs and sputters. The harbor is busy, and someone in a small boat sees your distress and tugs you ashore.

The splinter in the hull is significant but easily repaired. By the next morning, you are ready to embark on your mission again. You set out across the Channel.

On the beaches of Dunkirk, soldiers are spread out as far as you can see. They stand in lines, some of them in waist-deep water. Despite the conditions and the constant threat of attack, the soldiers are in good spirits, eager to be rescued.

More than 75 soldiers cram onto the yacht, and you set out back to England. There, the

Turn the page.

troops disembark, and you head to France again. Working alongside other small vessels and Navy ships, you carry another load of soldiers back.

Within a few days, more than 338,000 troops have been rescued from France. The evacuation is a success. The Allied troops have more fighting to do if they hope to defeat the Nazis, but you are proud of your role in the rescue.

THE END

To follow another path, turn to page 11.
To learn more about the Miracle of Dunkirk, turn to page 103.

"We need to keep going," you say.

"What good will a broken boat do us?" Williams mutters, but he doesn't argue any further.

You chug on in the direction of Dunkirk. On the horizon, you see plumes of smoke rising from the destroyed city. The beach is dark with thousands of soldiers awaiting evacuation. But then . . .

Chug. Chug. Splutter. Your boat wheezes and stops. You try to start it again, but the engine doesn't kick in.

"The hull is filling with water!" Williams yells from below.

You and Williams try to shovel out the water, but it's no use. The boat sinks. You and Williams cling to its frame, shouting for help.

At last, a fishing boat appears. The crew pulls Williams into the boat. Then, as they

Turn the page.

reach for you, the unmistakable siren of a Stuka fills the air.

You duck underwater as the plane dives toward the water. The blast of the bomb thrusts you down, deep into the water. You kick your feet and try to claw to the surface, but it's no use. Your chest almost bursts from lack of oxygen. Unable to hold your breath, you suck in a mouthful of water and sink all the way to the bottom, never to rise again.

THE END

To follow another path, turn to page 11.
To learn more about the Miracle of Dunkirk, turn to page 103.

“We’re doing one more trip,” you tell Rashad firmly.

He sighs. “Fine,” he says. “Just one more, though.”

You row toward the lines of soldiers waiting in the water, and pull them on one by one. When the boat is full, you start to row toward the *Basilisk*.

HMS *Basilisk*

Turn the page.

"Wait!" a voice yells.

You turn to see another soldier splashing toward you.

"Just one more!" he cries, lunging toward the lifeboat.

"We're full!" you tell him.

"You can take one more," he argues.

"If we let you on, we might capsize," Rashad says.

"Another lifeboat will come back for you!" you tell the soldier.

"He's just one more person," a soldier on board argues. "Let him on!"

"Yeah!" another soldier agrees.

You and Rashad look at each other. You don't want to risk tipping over, but the others in the boat want to let him on.

To let the soldier onboard, go to page 61.

To turn the soldier away, turn to page 63.

The soldier seems so desperate. You know you will feel guilty if you send him away.

"Come aboard," you say.

The soldiers in the lifeboat shift to find a place for the newcomer. You pull the soldier into the boat, and you and Rashad row toward the *Basilisk*.

The boat is steady, and you are happy with your decision. But then a larger boat passes, and its wake crashes against the lifeboat.

The boat rocks, and you cling to the hull. *Crash!* Another wave hits the lifeboat, and you tumble into the water.

When you splash to the surface, you see the lifeboat is overturned. Soldiers are flailing about in the water.

"Swim toward the boat!" you yell.

You grab hold of one soldier's arm and pull him to the lifeboat. Rashad does the same. But

Turn the page.

some of the men can't swim—there are some you can't save.

You and Rashad are able to flip the lifeboat upright. The surviving soldiers climb in. You row to the *Basilisk* with a lighter boat but a heavier heart. Onboard, many soldiers thank you for your part in rescuing them. But you feel guilty for those you couldn't save.

Nightmares chase you for years after the war. In 1957, 17 years after Operation Dynamo, you volunteer to help erect the Dunkirk Memorial. The memorial serves to remember those who were killed or lost during the evacuation. You hope the memorial helps keep the memory of the drowned soldiers alive.

THE END

To follow another path, turn to page 11.
To learn more about the Miracle of Dunkirk, turn to page 103.

You survey the boat again. The soldiers are jam-packed. There's no room for the soldier. The boat could sink.

"Sorry, mate. You'll have to wait for the next one," you say.

As you lean down to grab the oars, the soldier lunges angrily toward you. His fist connects with your chest. You go reeling and tumble into the water. Your head whacks the side of the boat as you fall.

The next thing you know, you're waking up onshore. A medic bends over you. He shines a light into your eyes and asks you to blink and look side to side.

"Clear," he says after you've complied.

"So I'm free to get back to my sailing duties?" you ask.

He shakes his head. "No. But you're free to join the lines of soldiers waiting for evacuation."

Turn the page.

Medics help an injured soldier in France during WWII.

"But—" you start to argue.

But the medic is already walking away. You scan the harbor. You see no sign of the lifeboat or the *Basilisk*. You have no choice but to step into line and wait for rescue.

THE END

To follow another path, turn to page 11.
To learn more about the Miracle of Dunkirk, turn to page 103.

Maybe Williams is right. You should continue to Dunkirk. There will be medics there to help the injured.

"Let's keep going," you say.

"We'll take turns piloting. While I steer, you can care for the injured," Williams says.

You agree. In the yacht's cabin, you find salve and bandages, and you treat the soldiers' wounds as best you can.

"We were on our way to England," one of the men grumbles in irritation. "Now we're going back to Dunkirk?"

You are trying to find comforting words when you hear Williams call from above. "Dunkirk in sight!"

You race to the deck. Ahead you see Dunkirk. The beaches are thick with thousands of soldiers, waiting to be evacuated. You can't believe how many troops are gathered. The lines stretch up and down the beaches.

Turn the page.

"We'll do our part, no matter how small," you say.

"Every little bit counts," Williams agrees.

When you reach Dunkirk, you transfer your wounded to a hospital ship. Then you pull alongside a Royal Navy vessel in the harbor and wait for orders.

A commander comes to the deck of the Navy ship. "This yacht is just what we needed!" he exclaims. "The Navy ships are too large to get close to the beaches. We can't load the troops."

You nod in understanding. A small yacht like yours can scoot into the shallow water, load men, and bring them to larger naval ships.

As you maneuver the yacht toward the beach, you hear a familiar whistle of a Stuka overhead. Quickly, you pull back on the rudder as the Stuka dives.

Whoosh! A bomb smacks the water. Debris hurtles through the air. A sharp pain runs down your shoulder as something hits you.

"Help! We've been hit!" a voice cries.

You turn to see a fishing boat listing to the side. Soldiers clutch the rails and scramble to stay on their feet. The boat is sinking fast.

Twisting the wheel, you turn the yacht toward the fishing boat. When you pull up alongside, you motion to the soldiers. "Jump aboard!"

Soldiers are rescued from the water after their craft was sunk during the Dunkirk operation.

Turn the page.

When your vessel is full, you sail the soldiers and crew to one of the waiting naval vessels. Then, you turn right back to the beach and gather another a group of men.

Over the next two days, you make several trips. Blessedly, clouds roll in, obscuring the Luftwaffe's aim, and threats from above lessen.

On the third day, you load a group of soldiers onto your yacht. This time, you are to take them across to England. Operation Dynamo is nearing an end.

The English Channel is calm that day. The trip goes quickly, without threat from above. When you reach Ramsgate, you are met with cheers from the harbor. You have played a heroic role in Operation Dynamo.

THE END

To follow another path, turn to page 11.
To learn more about the Miracle of Dunkirk, turn to page 103.

Rashad might be right—you both need to rest. You return to the *Basilisk*.

The soldiers onboard are tired but happy to finally be on a ship bound for England. One of them slaps you on the back.

"Thanks for rowing to get us, mate!" he says.

You smile and nod. You are tired too but happy with the work you have done.

While you and Rashad rest, other sailors take over. More soldiers are loaded onto the *Basilisk*. When the ship is full, the *Basilisk* begins its journey back across the English Channel with more than 300 soldiers in tow.

The soldiers get off at Dover, and the *Basilisk* heads back to Dunkirk. You and Rashad ready the lifeboat for another round of rescues.

"I'm heading to the boiler room to bring some food to my buddies before we set out," Rashad tells you.

Turn the page.

“All right,” you say. “The lifeboat is ready. Come back when we drop anchor.”

You rest on deck, watching the beaches grow closer. Suddenly, the sound of aircraft fills the air. It’s the Luftwaffe!

Bam! The blast knocks you off your feet. Your head smacks the lifeboat on the way down. Eventually, you pull yourself to your feet, feeling dazed. Sailors are rushing past.

“Where were we hit?” you ask one sailor.

“Below deck,” he says. “The boiler room.”

You clutch your head. Blood seeps through your fingers. You need to find Rashad.

You stumble below deck. Smoke fills your nostrils. “Rashad!” you call.

You make your way down the dark passage toward the boiler room. Other sailors push past you, carrying wounded soldiers in the opposite direction.

"Rashad!" you call again.

Then you see him staggering toward you. His face is burned and bloody. You catch him as he falls into you. Suddenly, another blast hits, knocking you and Rashad down. You tug his arm, but he doesn't move.

The ship lists sideways—it's sinking. You need to get on deck, fast. You can't carry Rashad by yourself, but you don't want to leave him. If you go up on deck, you might be able to find help.

To stay with Rashad, turn to page 72.

To return to deck and find help, turn to page 73.

"I'm not leaving you," you tell Rashad.

You stand up and stumble down the corridor, hoping to find someone to help. But no one else is below deck.

The swaying of the ship and your head injury make you dizzy. You return to Rashad and collapse next to him.

"We sure saved a lot of soldiers," you tell him as the world goes black.

THE END

To follow another path, turn to page 11.
To learn more about the Miracle of Dunkirk, turn to page 103.

You'll have better luck finding help on the top deck. So, even though the head injury makes you woozy, you make your way up.

"My partner is unconscious by the boiler room," you tell an officer. You don't hear his response—everything goes dark as you faint.

When you come to, you are on board the HMS *Whitehall.* You look around quickly, but you don't see Rashad. Your heart plummets.

You learn that after the bombing, the *Whitehall* came to the *Basilisk*'s aid, rescuing you, along with eight officers and 123 crew. Rashad was not among them.

The *Whitehall* takes you and the others to Dover, where you board another ship bound for Dunkirk. The war—and rescue—are still ongoing. You vow to save more soldiers in Rashad's memory.

THE END

To follow another path, turn to page 11.
To learn more about the Miracle of Dunkirk, turn to page 103.

Chapter 4

SPITFIRES AND HURRICANES

The sky over Horsham airfield in Norfolk, England, is blue and sunny—a perfect day for flying. When the RAF commander calls a meeting, you hope it means you'll be flying some practice drills today. But the commander has other plans.

"You will be flying an important mission," he says. "We will be providing air support for Operation Dynamo—a daring rescue to evacuate our soldiers trapped in France."

Your entire life, you dreamed of becoming a fighter pilot. After high school, you enlisted in the British Royal Air Force. When you passed basic training, you went on to flight school, where you learned to fly various types of planes.

Turn the page.

Then, you continued to combat training, learning tactics to engage and fight enemy aircraft.

"The situation in France is dire," the commander explains.

You learn that Nazis have surrounded more than 300,000 BEF in Dunkirk, France. The Royal Navy needs to get the soldiers out and soon.

"That's where you come in," your commander continues. "The Luftwaffe will be attacking soldiers on the beaches and ships in the English Channel. You will need to provide air coverage for the operation, shooting down enemy planes before they can attack."

Your heart speeds up at the thought of being part of such a huge rescue mission. This is the moment you've been waiting for.

"The RAF is stretched thin," your commander says. "We are training new recruits as fast as we can. But you may be outnumbered in the air."

"We'll still take the enemy down!" your pal Chaz exclaims.

"They're no match for us!" you agree.

The next days are spent preparing. You'll be lifting off from Hornchurch, a small airfield east of London.

To combat the German Luftwaffe, the RAF will need its best planes. Two fighter planes stand out above the rest: the Supermarine Spitfire and the Hawker Hurricane. Both are single-seater fighter planes, but they have some differences. The Spitfire is speedy and agile, good at intercepting enemy fighters. The Hurricane, meanwhile, is sturdier and can better withstand attacks.

To fly a Spitfire, turn to page 78.

To take the controls of a Hurricane, turn to page 80.

Your day begins at 3:00 a.m. You gulp down some coffee and head to the tarmac where the Spitfires are warming up, their engines roaring. Flames from the exhaust light up the dark field.

You hurry toward your Spitfire and climb into the cockpit, adjusting your helmet and checking the controls. Then you lift off, following your squadron leader Bryant in formation.

A British Spitfire waits on an airstrip.

The Spitfire's see-through dome offers a great view. The clouds seem to part as you weave through, getting into formation. The only thing you don't love about the Spitfire is the lack of hindsight. In order to see clearly behind you, you have to weave back and forth.

As you fly over the English Channel, you catch a glimpse of an aircraft to the north. You speed up, but can't tell if the plane is enemy or friendly.

To go after him and find out, you'd have to break formation. If it's an enemy plane, this is your chance to head him off before he can attack the ground troops. But you're not sure you want to break formation on your very first flight of the mission. Maybe it's better to stay in formation and radio your squadron leader.

To break formation and chase the plane,
turn to page 81.

To stay in formation and radio your squadron leader,
turn to page 82.

The Spitfire is fast, but the Hurricane is more reliable. The sky is still dark as you head to the tarmac at 3:00 a.m. The Hurricanes are warming up, their engines loud in the quiet before dawn.

Giving Chaz a thumbs-up, you climb into the Hurricane's cockpit. At the signal from the squadron leader, you lift off, heading for the skies above Dunkirk.

Then, the squadron leader comes on the radio. "We're going to split into two groups. One will fly directly over Dunkirk to protect it. The other will circle Dunkirk to head off any Nazis that are heading that way."

Chaz radios you. "Well? Which way should we go?"

To fly directly over Dunkirk, turn to page 87.

To circle Dunkirk, turn to page 89.

Touching the controls just lightly, you zoom away from your group and veer north, toward the the other aircraft. Clouds obscure your vision, then you spot the craft ahead. You dart through the clouds, giving full chase.

Then, he's gone.

You dip below the clouds, but there's no plane in sight, just the large expanse of water below. You are still north of Dunkirk. You have two choices—you could turn back to rejoin your squadron. Or, you could continue toward Dunkirk, searching for the plane.

To return to your squadron, turn to page 92.

To continue toward Dunkirk and search for the plane, turn to page 94.

With every passing second, the plane is getting farther away, but you decide to stay in formation. That way you'll have backup.

You radio your squadron leader and tell him where you saw the plane.

"Follow me," Bryant says, shifting direction.

You and your squadron follow. Soon, a Nazi Messerschmitt fighter plane is in your sights.

"Enemy spotted!" Bryant says over the radio.

He zooms toward the plane. But suddenly, several more Nazi planes appear. You zigzag out of their reach. Behind you, another RAF pilot fires, taking down one of the Nazi planes.

You swivel back around, giving another Messerschmitt full chase. You're on his back in no time. When you are close enough, you fire.

Bam! You see the other cockpit fill with smoke. The pilot bails out. His parachute blossoms open as he falls toward the water.

The other Messerschmitts veer off into the distance. Bryant leads the formation on to Dunkirk. As you approach, you look down at the massive operation. Hundreds of thousands of soldiers cram the beaches. There are so many people that you can't even see the sand.

Out in the Channel, Navy ships move toward Dunkirk. It will take days to get everyone off the beach. You are glad the RAF is there to help fend off German attacks.

"Heading back to Hornchurch airfield," Bryant radios.

The sky above Dunkirk is free of enemy traffic, but you don't feel ready to go back just yet. You check your gauges. You have enough fuel left for another patrol over the beach.

To return to Hornchurch with your squadron, turn to page 84.

To conduct another patrol on your own, turn to page 97.

You'd like to do one more patrol, but staying with your squadron is your best bet. You fall into formation, and in less than an hour, you are back on solid ground.

In early evening, your squadron heads out again. This time, the sun is setting behind you. The skies are quiet except for the roar of the Spitfire's engines.

But as you approach Dunkirk, you hear the screech of Nazi Stuka dive-bombers. Their formation appears. They are about to hit Dunkirk.

"Moving in for the attack," Bryant says over the radio.

A Spitfire flies through the sky.

Your group surges toward the Stukas, breaking apart their formation. The sky is now a mess of planes, all zigzagging through the air.

You twist through the chaos, peppering the enemy planes with bullets. A Stuka fires back, and a sudden jolt sends you flying forward in the cockpit.

"You've been hit!" a pilot named Stan radios. "I'm coming in. Bail out!"

Your engine hisses and sputters. You see Stan hurtling toward you. The Stuka is just about to fire off another round when Stan blasts him.

As your engine sputters again, you open the cockpit and jump, pulling the cord of your parachute once you're free of the plane. The chute opens, and you drift down, landing on the soft sand near the Channel.

You aren't far from the beaches of Dunkirk. You see soldiers gathered for rescue. Little boats

Turn the page.

zoom in, gathering the men and taking them to larger ships farther from shore.

You make your way toward the groups of soldiers. "I'm a pilot," you say when you reach them. "I was hit and had to bail out."

One of the soldiers shrugs. "You're gonna have to wait in line like the rest of us."

The lines are so long, you feel as though you'll never get back to base. For two days, you stand on the beaches, dropping to the ground when Stuka dive-bombers come close. You wish you could be up there fending them off.

At last, it's your turn. You climb on a little boat with the soldiers. You are all to be brought back to England, then return to fight the Nazis again.

THE END

To follow another path, turn to page 11.
To learn more about the Miracle of Dunkirk, turn to page 103.

You and Chaz join the group heading directly for Dunkirk. The day is cloudy, and the skies are deserted. The cloud cover must have scared away any Nazi planes.

You radio Chaz. “I guess we chose wrong.”

“No action today,” Chaz agrees.

The squadron leader drops down below cloud level to gain a better view of Dunkirk. You and the others follow, and you get your first glimpse of the rescue.

The operation is immense. Hundreds of thousands of soldiers wait on the beaches. Navy ships wait in the Channel. Little boats scurry to shore to gather soldiers and take them to the waiting ships.

You’re more grateful than ever for the cloud cover. With clearer skies, Nazis would have no problem dropping bombs.

Bam. Bam-bam!

Turn the page.

The noise rains down from above. You glance up and see a Nazi plane dropping straight toward you, its guns aimed at your Hurricane.

You have to act fast. You swivel the control stick, and the Hurricane darts into the clouds just in time. The clouds are thick, and you see no sign of Chaz. You reach for the radio.

"Chaz?" you say. All you hear is silence. The radio must be busted.

Then the cockpit fills with fumes. You've been hit.

You think fast. You could crash land in France and hope to find safety with French troops. But you risk being caught by Germans. Or you could splash down into the Channel and hope that the British Navy sees you and picks you up.

To crash land in France, turn to page 91.

To splash down into the Channel, turn to page 98.

The idea of heading off the Germans appeals to you. You and Chaz join the group circling the airspace around Dunkirk.

At first, the sky is empty of any planes except your Hurricane squadron. Then, from the east, a pack of Nazi planes thunders toward you.

You veer out of formation to avoid a hit. Chaz follows. Soon the sky is swirling with planes—British Hurricanes and Nazi Stukas.

British Hurricanes fly in formation, preparing to defend against German attacks in the sky.

Turn the page.

Catching one in your sight, you fire, but the Stuka swerves just in time. You miss.

The Stuka swirls on you, but Chaz is right there. He blasts the German plane, and it spins to earth.

"Thanks, buddy," you radio.

Chaz doesn't reply. You see another Stuka bearing down on him. You spin to catch it in your sights, but the Stuka juts away. Chaz chases it out of sight.

The air is suddenly calm.

"Chaz?" you radio.

There's no answer. You try again, but all you hear is silence.

You check your fuel gauges. You're getting low. You need to get back to base soon. But you don't want to leave Chaz.

To head back to the base in England, turn to page 99.

To find Chaz, turn to page 101.

You don't want to risk drowning in the Channel, so you turn toward land. The engine sputters. The plane is descending fast.

As the plane hits rough air, you lurch in your seat. You drop the flaps and lower the landing gear, trying to maintain calm.

You land on an expanse of farm field. The plane skids to a stop. Hurriedly, you jump out, in case the plane blows up.

Suddenly, a group of soldiers bursts from a grove of trees, their guns aimed at you. Your heart plummets to your feet. Nazis!

The soldiers take you to a German prisoner of war camp. Your days are filled with forced marches and hunger. You don't even know that the Dunkirk evacuation was a success until the war finally ends and you are released from camp.

THE END

To follow another path, turn to page 11.
To learn more about the Miracle of Dunkirk, turn to page 103.

You turn back to rejoin your group. As you come up behind the formation, you radio the squadron leader. He's not happy.

"You shouldn't go off on your own," Bryant chides. "We need every plane we can get."

The Spitfires thunder over the Channel toward Dunkirk. Suddenly, you no longer have the skies to yourselves. A formation of planes appears straight ahead.

"12 Messerschmitts!" Bryant calls over the radio. "Get ready!"

The Germans see you coming. They split from their neat formations and weave haphazardly through the air.

You get on the tail of one of the Messerschmitts. When you catch it in your sights, you press the firing button. *Bam!* Its engine stops, and you fire another stream of bullets. The plane plummets and crashes.

Your heart gives a whirl of excitement. But your excitement fades as you look around and realize that half your squadron is gone—so are the other Messerschmitts.

"Bryant?" you say over the radio.

Another pilot, Stan, answers. "He's gone. Nazis got him and three others."

You swallow hard. You join what's left of the crew and head back to Hornchurch.

"At least we took down some Nazis," you say as you walk across the tarmac.

Stan shakes his head. "Not enough. Those Messerschmitts that got away dropped bombs on Dunkirk. Blew up a Navy destroyer."

Sadness and disappointment overwhelm you. Even though you took down a plane, the mission is a failure.

THE END

To follow another path, turn to page 11.
To learn more about the Miracle of Dunkirk, turn to page 103.

You don't want to return until you have succeeded in taking down the German plane.

"On the hunt for a plane spotted over the Channel," you radio to your squadron leader.

"We were wondering where you were," Bryant says. "Keep on the hunt. We'll be coming up behind you shortly."

You slow your speed and glide through the sky, scanning the horizon for any sign of the plane. All is clear, though.

Suddenly, a plane appears on your left. You bear down, ready to give chase. As you approach, another plane appears, then another and another. It's the Luftwaffe!

You quickly count—eight planes to your one. You hope your squadron arrives soon. Until then, you're on your own.

You speed toward the German formation, darting up and over. The Spitfire is quick,

An RAF Spitfire attacks German Stuka dive-bombers.

and even if the Nazis see you, they don't break formation. They might be more intent on attacking Dunkirk than on chasing a single plane.

This is your chance. You circle back toward the formation. One plane spots you, breaking away from the group, but you are ready. You fire at him. It's a hit! The craft falls to earth in a fiery spiral, disappearing into the water below.

Turn the page.

Then, you see your squadron approaching. They zoom toward you, and you and the others overtake the Nazi formation. Two more hits take down two planes, and the Nazis turn away, disappearing into the clouds.

As you head back to the airfield, you feel a sense of pride. You helped your squadron take down three Nazi planes, saving Dunkirk from their attack. You are ready to do it again tomorrow.

Over the next several days, you conduct missions in the air over Dunkirk. After nine days, the evacuation mission ends. More than 338,000 soldiers have been rescued from France. The strength of the British Army has been preserved, with help from you and the Royal Air Force.

THE END

To follow another path, turn to page 11.
To learn more about the Miracle of Dunkirk, turn to page 103.

Curiosity and excitement win out. You leave the formation and circle the skies over Dunkirk.

Clouds have rolled in, and you dip below to gain a better view. As you lift back up, a sudden jerk on your tail sends you sideways.

Quickly, you right the plane, then weave to look behind. Uh-oh. An enemy plane is chasing you. And worse, you've been hit. Tendrils of smoke rise from the left wing flap.

You bank hard to the right, hoping your sudden turn throws the enemy off. But the hit has slowed you down. With your left wing damaged, you can't weave as fast as you want to.

The Nazi gains on you and fires again. This time, the bullets puncture the fuselage. The Spitfire explodes before you have time to bail, and you go down into the English Channel.

THE END

To follow another path, turn to page 11.
To learn more about the Miracle of Dunkirk, turn to page 103.

With so many Germans in France, landing there is risky. You decide to take your chances with the English Channel.

Engine chugging, you descend toward the water. Then you see the gunners on a destroyer raise their guns at you.

No! They think you're an enemy plane!

You brace for the bullets, but none come. Just in time, the gunners see that the plane is an RAF Hurricane.

The plane splashes down into the Channel, and you crawl out. A boat races toward you, and the crew pulls you in. You are wet and cold but alive.

You are taken to a Navy destroyer filled with evacuated soldiers. The destroyer takes you and the soldiers back to England. In just two days, you are back on duty, ready to fly again over Dunkirk.

THE END

To follow another path, turn to page 11.
To learn more about the Miracle of Dunkirk, turn to page 103.

You can't risk running out of fuel. The British Army needs to be evacuated, and you and your plane are an important piece of the rescue mission.

You turn back toward England. The fuel gauge drops, but you make it to Hornchurch airfield in the nick of time.

Your squadron leader greets you as you step out of the Hurricane.

"Did Chaz make it back?" you ask.

He shakes his head. Chaz is gone.

The sun is bright in your face as tears fill your eyes. You adjust your goggles and nod.

"He saved me," you say. "Chaz died a hero."

Over the next days of the rescue, you shoot down four Nazi planes. You dedicate your missions to Chaz. You know he would be proud.

Turn the page.

RAF airmen flew thousands of missions at Dunkirk, gathering information and providing air support for troops on the beaches, as well as those on ships.

By the end of the rescue, more than 338,000 soldiers are evacuated from Dunkirk. The mission is a success, and you and the RAF played a part.

THE END

To follow another path, turn to page 11.
To learn more about the Miracle of Dunkirk, turn to page 103.

You have just enough fuel to circle the skies one more time. As you do, you desperately scan the air around you for Chaz. You radio him again, but there is no answer.

Finally, you accept that you have to go back without him. As you turn toward England, you see a dark dot to your right. Could it be Chaz?

The plane speeds toward you. Your chest tightens as you realize that it's a Nazi Stuka.

You speed up, but the Stuka catches you. A blast of bullets hits your plane. Your last thought before the engine explodes is that you hope Chaz fared better than you.

THE END

To follow another path, turn to page 11.
To learn more about the Miracle of Dunkirk, turn to page 103.

Chapter 5

MIRACLE OF DUNKIRK

Operation Dynamo began on May 26, 1940. The goal was to evacuate at least 45,000 troops from the beaches of Dunkirk, France, in two days. There was a reason for the tight timeline—British commanders thought that within two days, Nazi attacks would compromise the rescue.

But on May 24, the Nazis stopped their ground attack through France. They wanted to save manpower and weapons. This gave the British Royal Navy more time.

During the operation, the Royal Air Force helped to fend off attacking German aircraft. Cloudy conditions also kept the Luftwaffe from landing strikes. This—along with the courage of the soldiers, the Royal Navy, and the RAF—helped the mission to succeed.

One Navy sailor who took part in the evacuation was Reg Vine. Vine was only 15 years old when he went to Dunkirk as a sea cadet. He was sent on a launch named *Rummy II* and didn't know about the rescue mission until he was at sea. Over two days, Vine rowed a lifeboat, making many trips to carry soldiers from the shore to the launch.

Harold "Vic" Viner was a beachmaster whose job was to maintain order on the beaches at Dunkirk. He was ordered to shoot anyone who fought or tried to cut in line. His brother, Albert, was on the destroyer

The HMS *Grenade*, part of the British Royal Navy

HMS *Grenade*. From shore, Vic watched in horror as Stukas attacked the *Grenade*. Albert survived but was later killed on the HMS *Crested Eagle*.

Flying Officer Michael Lyne was stationed at Horsham airfield when he was called to the Dunkirk evacuation. From Hornchurch he flew a Spitfire to Dunkirk. On one patrol he was shot by a Messerschmitt. His engine failing, he had to decide whether to splash down in the English Channel, crash land in France, or try to return to England. He barely made it to England and crash landed on a beach.

In a little more than a week, more than 338,000 Allied soldiers were evacuated from the coast of France—far more than the 45,000 expected. Still, more than 50,000 British troops were unable to escape. Much heavy equipment had to be left behind. Tanks, weapons, and artillery were abandoned.

Even with the losses, the evacuation was a success. Because so many troops were evacuated, it became known as the Miracle of Dunkirk. Returning soldiers were greeted with cheers. Britain was inspired to continue fighting the war. On June 4, British Prime Minister Winston Churchill gave a famous speech, telling the public, "We shall fight on the beaches . . . we shall never surrender."

The evacuation of Dunkirk was a turning point in the war effort. The BEF returned to the continent of Europe to fight against the Nazis. The Allied powers grew to include the United States, Soviet Union, and China, among others. The Axis powers grew too. Italy and Japan joined the Nazis.

The war raged on. On September 2, 1945, World War II officially ended in an Allied victory. The victory was made possible by the many soldiers who endured the conditions at Dunkirk and lived to fight another day.

MORE ABOUT OPERATION DYNAMO

››› The British Royal Navy began planning Operation Dynamo on May 20, 1940, from the Royal Navy headquarters at Dover Castle. Vice Admiral Bertram Ramsay planned and commanded the operation from Dover. He and his staff worked around the clock for nine days. For Ramsay's role, King George VI made him Knight Commander.

››› Captain William Tennant oversaw Operation Dynamo on the ground. On May 27, Tennant arrived in Dunkirk, France, and saw that the Luftwaffe had destroyed Dunkirk's port. He determined that soldiers would need to be evacuated from shallow beaches or from the mole—a 0.8 mile (1.3 kilometer) long pier jutting into the water. But the water was too shallow for large naval vessels to get close. The British Ministry of Shipping telephoned boat builders, asking them to collect all boats that could navigate shallow waters. More than 1,000 watercraft were involved in the evacuation. Approximately 700 were civilian crafts.

››› At 10:50 p.m. June 2, Tennant radioed Admiral Ramsay, declaring that all BEF had been evacuated. Over the next two days, other Allied forces were evacuated. In total, Operation Dynamo saved about 338,000 troops—198,000 BEF and 140,000 Allied troops, mostly French.

››› Around 240 ships were lost and 45 damaged over the course of Operation Dynamo. The Royal Air Force lost 84 planes. More than 50,000 British troops were left behind following the rescue. Of these, 11,000 were killed. Most of the rest were captured and became prisoners of war who were released when WWII was over.

KEY RESCUE EQUIPMENT

a British RAF Spitfire

HMS *Albury*, part of the British Royal Navy, carried more than 1,800 soldiers safely back to England during Operation Dynamo.

TIMELINE OF EVENTS

SEPTEMBER 1, 1939—German Nazi forces, under the command of Adolf Hitler, invade Poland.

SEPTEMBER 3, 1939—Great Britain and France declare war on Germany.

MAY 10, 1940—Nazis invade Belgium, the Netherlands, and France.

MAY 20, 1940—British military commanders begin planning Operation Dynamo in order to get British troops out of France.

MAY 26, 1940—Under British Prime Minister Winston Churchill's orders, Operation Dynamo officially begins at 7:00 p.m.

MAY 26–JUNE 4, 1940—On the first full day of the operation, 7,669 troops are rescued. By the end, more than 1,000 vessels rescue 338,000 troops from the beaches of Dunkirk.

JUNE–DECEMBER 1941—Axis powers attack the Soviet Union. The Soviet Union enters the war on the Allied side.

DECEMBER 7, 1941—Japanese planes bomb Pearl Harbor in Hawaii. One day later, the United States joins the Allied powers.

JUNE 6, 1944—Allied forces storm the beaches of Normandy, France, which is under German control.

DECEMBER 16, 1944—Germans launch a surprise attack, resulting in the Battle of the Bulge. The Germans lose the battle and retreat.

APRIL 30, 1945—Allied forces close in on Berlin, Germany. Hitler dies by suicide.

MAY 7, 1945—Germany surrenders.

AUGUST 1945—The U.S. drops atomic bombs on Hiroshima and Nagasaki, Japan.

SEPTEMBER 2, 1945—Japan surrenders, ending World War II.

GLOSSARY

artillery (ar-TI-luhr-ee)—cannons and other large guns used during battles

boiler (BOY-luhr)—a tank that boils water to produce steam

civilian (si-VIL-yuhn)—a person who is not in the military

dictator (DIK-tay-tuhr)—someone who has complete control of a country, often ruling it unjustly

delirium (dih-LEER-ee-uhm)—a mental disturbance marked by confusion, disturbed speech, and hallucinations

evacuate (i-VA-kyuh-wayt)—to leave an area during a time of danger

formation (for-MAY-shuhn)—a group of airplanes flying together in a pattern

hull (HUHL)—the frame or body of a boat

panzer (PAN-zur)—a German tank of World War II

recruit (ri-KROOT)—a new member of the armed forces

salve (SAV)—a thick medicine or lotion that relieves pain and helps heal wounds or burns

shrapnel (SHRAP-nuhl)—pieces that have broken off from an explosive shell

squadron (SKWAHD-ruhn)—an official military unit

steamer (STEE-mer)—a ship driven by steam

yacht (YOT)—a large boat or small ship used for sailing or racing

READ MORE

Doeden, Matt. *What If You Were on the European Front in World War II?: An Interactive History Adventure.* North Mankato, MN: Capstone Press, 2023.

Lassieur, Allison. *Surviving the Blitz of World War II: A History-Seeking Adventure.* North Mankato, MN: Capstone Press, 2025.

Roberts, Kelly. *World War II: What Can We Learn from the People Who Witnessed War?* Shrewsbury, Shropshire, England: Cheriton Children's Books, 2025.

INTERNET SITES

Britannica Kids: Dunkirk Evacuation
kids.britannica.com/kids/article/Dunkirk-evacuation/623980

Kiddle: Dunkirk Evacuation Facts for Kids
kids.kiddle.co/Dunkirk_evacuation

Social Studies for Kids: The Dunkirk Evacuation
socialstudiesforkids.com/articles/worldhistory/dunkirkevacuation.htm

ABOUT THE AUTHOR

Jessica Gunderson grew up in the small town of Washburn, North Dakota. She has a bachelor's degree from the University of North Dakota and an MFA in Creative Writing from Minnesota State University, Mankato. She has written more than one hundred books for young readers. Her book *President Lincoln's Killer and the America He Left Behind* won a 2018 Eureka! Nonfiction Children's Book Silver Award. She currently lives in Madison, Wisconsin.

MORE BOOKS IN THIS SERIES

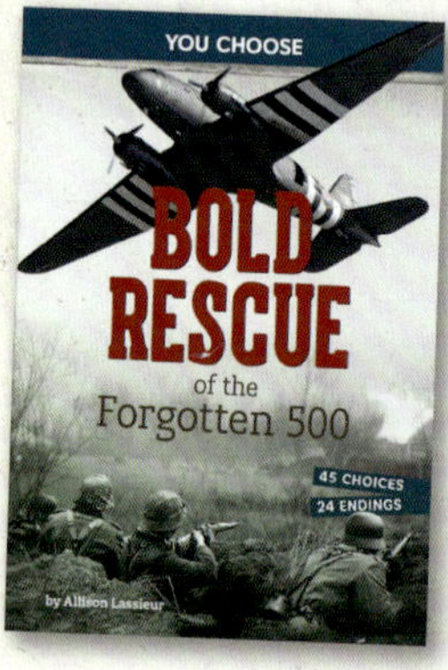

YOU CHOOSE
BOLD RESCUE of the Forgotten 500
45 CHOICES
24 ENDINGS
by Allison Lassieur

YOU CHOOSE
BRAVE ESCAPES from Stalag Luft I
39 CHOICES
21 ENDINGS
by Eric Braun

YOU CHOOSE
DANGEROUS RESCUE from Amiens Prison
31 CHOICES
14 ENDINGS
by Matt Doeden